GRETCHEN
GILLFILLAN

MH

THE
STORY OF
CAKE

THE STORY OF

CAKE

NORAH SMARIDGE

Abingdon
Nashville

THE STORY OF CAKE

Copyright © 1978 by Abingdon

Library of Congress Cataloging in Publication Data

SMARIDGE, NORAH.
  The story of cake.
  SUMMARY. Traces the history of the cake including the birthday cake, doughnuts, and cake mixes. Provides recipes for such treats as gingerbread, fruitcake, American crumb cake, and Old World honey cake.
  1. Cake—Juvenile literature.   [1. Cake. 2. Baking]   I. Title.
TX771.S43   641.8'653   78-24069

ISBN 0-687-39660-3

For Scott and Kelli Smaridge, with love

Acknowledgments

The recipe for Minty's Fruitcake on p. 76 is from *Piccolo Eating Book* by Bronwen O'Connor, published by Pan Books Ltd., London. Copyright © Bronwen O'Connor 1976. Used by permission.

The recipe for Sugar Balls on p. 77 is from *Crazy Quilt Cookery*. Used by permission of Bunny Day.

The recipe for Date Nut Squares on p. 53, and five recipes for cakes made from mixes on pp. 86-90 are from *Cookie Craft* and *Quick'n Tasty*. Used by permission of General Mills, Inc.

Contents

Preface 11
One. Ashcakes, Anyone? 15
Two. Coffee Rings and Fruitcake 19
Three. Sugar Makes Its Bow 25
Four. Fit for a Feast Day 28
Five. Birthday Cake, with Candles 33
Six. Love's Old, Sweet Cake 39
Seven. The Super-Cakes: Cheesecake and Gingerbread 42
Eight. Cakes in the New World 47
Nine. Enter the Layer Cake 51
Ten. From Angel to Devil 54
Eleven. More American Cakes 57
Twelve. The Magical Cake Mix 61
Thirteen. What's in a Cake Name? 64
Fourteen. Old and New Recipes 68
Index 94

Preface

Cake, in its hundreds of delicious varieties, is eaten the world over by many people. Recipes for simple and elaborate cakes abound and continue to multiply. Entire cookbooks have been devoted to this mouth-watering food, with recipes for everything from breakfast cakes to cake-based desserts.

Yet surprisingly little is known about how and where cake got its start, and how it spread and developed down through the ages. This book unravels the history of cake, beginning with the ashcakes of biblical times and ending with the commercial cake mixes so popular today.

THE STORY OF CAKE

one
Ashcakes, Anyone?

Although cake of many kinds has been a favorite food for thousands of years, the mystery of who invented it has yet to be solved. Some historians say that Thearion, a Sicilian baker, concocted the first cake in the fifth century before Christ. Others claim that the Egyptians made something very like coffee rings at least four thousand years earlier.

In all probability cake of some sort was eaten as far back as primitive times. Even in the early Stone Age, man knew how to grind corn between two stones. He knew how to build a fire and how to rob a beehive. So, when he tired of eating grubs and shellfish and hairy caterpillars, what was more natural than to mix some of his cornmeal with honey and make himself a cake?

In Old Testament times, Hebrew women baked daily and made a crude sort of cake as well as bread. Unlike today's women, they had to start from scratch by grinding their own wheat or barley. This was a difficult process, during which they squatted on the

15

ground and pounded the grain with a pestle into a stone-hard vessel.

When the grain was coarsely ground, they mixed it with water and salt and turned it into dough. Cake was less trouble than bread to make because the dough for bread-making had to be set aside overnight or until it rose. But cakes made from the dough could be baked and eaten right away.

The whole family helped with the baking chores. While one woman ground the corn, another mixed the dough. Still another patted it into loaves and carried them to the oven. The children were kept busy gathering wood and refueling the oven, which at first was not much more than a shallow bowl turned upside down on the fire and resting on three or four stones. A second kind of oven was made out of a large earthenware jar, plastered with mud, with a fire inside and a hole in the top. When the fire died down, the women popped thin sheets of dough on to the hot inner surface of the oven where they stuck until they were baked.

Though bread was baked every day, cakes were made only for festive occasions. They could not have been much tastier than bread. Sometimes the dough was mixed with oil to make it a little richer. Sometimes the cakes were cooked in oil. And sometimes the dough was flattened into thin wafers and spread with honey.

Although they were not very appetizing, cakes were often presented as gifts. When Jeroboam, the first king of the ten tribes of Israel, wanted to know whether his sick son would recover, he sent his wife to the prophet Ahijah with "ten loaves, and cracknels, and a cruse of honey." The cracknels were probably small cakes, sprinkled with seeds. These cakes have a long history. They are still eaten in England, where they are known as puff cracknels and are so dry that they have to be piled with jelly to get them down.

Country dwellers in the Bible lands turned their dough into

ashcakes. They shaped it into thin pancakes and baked them on stones heated by a wood-and-dung fire and thickly covered with ashes. Abraham served these to the three angels who, disguised as travelers, brought him a message from God. He was sitting at the opening of his tent, on the plain of Mamre, when he saw the three strangers approaching. Running to meet them, he begged them to sit down and rest while he got them food and drink. Then he hurried into his tent, calling to his wife, Sarah, "Quickly take three measures of fine meal and bake cakes upon the hearth."

While Sarah was busy making the ashcakes, Abraham went back to the three strangers with butter, milk, and meat from a tender calf. The angels then gave him good tidings. Abraham and his wife, now old, believed that they would never have a child. But now one of the angels told Abraham, "Sarah, thy wife, shall have a son."

Ashcakes also appear in a story about the great prophet Elijah. During the reign of the evil Queen Jezebel, who persecuted those who believed in God, Elijah took refuge in the desert near the brook named Cherith. Ravens brought him bread and meat, and he drank cool, sweet water from the spring. When the water dried up, he journeyed to Zarephath, where he saw a woman gathering sticks near the gate of the city. "Fetch me, I beg you, a little water," he called to her, "and bring me a morsel of bread."

The woman turned to him in distress. "As the Lord your God knows, I have only a handful of meal in a barrel and a little oil in a jar. As you see, I am gathering two sticks, that I may go in and prepare it for myself and my son, so that we may eat it and die."

Elijah spoke to her kindly. "Do not fear. Go and do as you have said, but first make me a little cake." The woman did so and was well rewarded. Not only was there enough cake left for them, but from then on her supply of meal and oil never ran out.

Up to that time, cakes were simply a mixture of crude flour and water, with sometimes a little oil. Then an unknown genius got the idea of using honey as an ingredient instead of just spreading it on thin wafers. It is strange that honey was not used in this way much earlier because it was one of the best known and most enjoyable foods of early man. The thick syrup, product of the wild bee, was plentiful in regions like the Bible lands, where flowers flourished and the climate was dry and warm. Honey was always in demand and was traded widely by the nomads of the deserts.

The new ingredient made a great difference to cake-baking. From that time on, cakes became sweeter and richer tasting and began to be baked in greater variety.

two
Coffee Rings and Fruitcake

Although the Chinese probably baked cakes and pastries several thousand years before the time of Christ, we get our first knowledge of the art of baking from the Egyptians. They outdid the Israelites in the variety and richness of their cakes.

The Nile River valley was so fertile that it was easy for the Egyptians to grow large crops of fine grain. Both bread and cake were taken seriously.

Stone tablets on graves reveal that the early Egyptians believed cake to be essential not only in this life but in the life after death. A wealthy man would ask for more than a dozen kinds of cake to accompany him to the next world. They would be put in his tomb along with bread and other foodstuffs. The oldest bread, found by archaeologists in Egyptian tombs, is over five thousand years old.

The Egyptians were so fond of cake themselves that they were sure their gods, too, would relish this delicious food. So cakes were often offered on pagan altars. Some of them were very

imaginative. Their sacred bull Apis, for instance, was appeased with an offering of cakes with honeyed horns. Rameses III, founder of the twelfth dynasty of Egyptian kings and a brilliant ruler, flooded the temples of his gods with cake. In a single year, he sacrificed some nine thousand cakes and twenty thousand loaves of bread.

In addition to the plain cake that they ate every day, the Egyptians made nut cakes, using the walnuts that grew in Mediterranean lands.

Seed cake was another favorite. Dr. Ralph Lee, an engineer with a keen interest in the history of baking, proved this recently during a meeting of the American Society of Baking Engineers. He had an Egyptian papyrus, at least six thousand years old, which pictured bakers taking cakes from the oven and sprinkling them with seeds. The Egyptians, no doubt, also invented ring-shaped cakes, because the same papyrus showed dozens of ring-shaped cakes hanging on the bakery walls.

The Egyptians baked the first of the dark fruitcakes that have become a Christmas treat in many lands. The homemaker in the Nile Valley had no bakery where beautifully packaged fruitcakes could be bought. She and her family had to make their own. They ground the wheat into flour. They gathered rare spices. They picked the tropical fruits—apricots, pomegranates, grapes, dates, figs—and preserved them by drying them in the sun. With these ingredients, plus oil and honey, they made the first fruitcakes.

Similar cakes were made later in Rome and Spain. Centuries after this, British sailors, returning from oriental ports and foreign lands, told stories about the wonderful fruit-filled cakes they had eaten there. Their wives urged them to bring back the ingredients, and they did—currants and raisins from Greece and Turkey; almonds from Spain; citrus peel, preserved in honey, from Italy. From the Orient they brought strange seeds and bits of tree bark that, when pounded in a mortar, gave a pleasant, spicy flavor to the cakes.

As these ingredients became known, they were made into trade items and sold to raise money for seafaring expeditions. British bakers, tasting the fruitcakes in sailors' homes, soon learned the recipe and began to make them for sale.

Glacé, or sugar iced, fruits were sometimes used for decoration. The first record we have of such fruit goes back to the time of Marco Polo, the famous Venetian traveler. While in China, he and his companions used to extract sugar syrup from cane or bamboo and soak their ginger, kumquats, and other Oriental fruits in it to make them soft and sweet.

When a baker perfected a recipe to his satisfaction, that particular recipe would be jealously guarded so that nobody could steal the secret. The precious recipes were handed down from one generation of bakers to the next and were eventually brought to America.

American bakers found ways of making the fruitcake even more delicious. They refined the ingredients and used a wider selection of nuts. Research developed ways of preserving fruits and the flavorings from spices, herbs, and roots.

Both light and dark fruitcakes are made today, the lighter kind containing more cherries, pineapple, and white raisins and little or no molasses. The cakes come in all sizes and shapes, sometimes decorated with candied fruit or mouth-watering icings.

three
Sugar Makes Its Bow

During the Middle Ages, about 1000 to 1400, people tried many new ingredients in their cakes. Sixteenth-century bakers gave them a touch of color with saffron, an orange-yellowy flavoring extracted from the autumn crocus.

In the monasteries, when the monks got tired of eating little fried cakes as a supper treat, they began to look around the monastery garden with new interest. Surely some of these flowers and bright berries would make a tasty addition to cake. The monks mashed raspberries and parsnips and added them to the cake mixture with pleasing results. They crushed violets and used them to give fragrance. (Crystallized violets are still used as decorations on iced cakes.) They even made cakes from sorrel, an acid-leaved herb.

Even with these improvements, cakes were a long way from our chocolate layers, angel food cake, and luscious cream puffs.

23

Nothing really startling happened to cakes until sugar made its bow.

The Crusaders, Christian warriors who went on expeditions to recover the Holy Land from the Muhammadans, learned about sugar and brought samples back to Europe. During the thirteenth, fourteenth, and fifteenth centuries it remained a luxury that only kings and nobility could afford. When the Portuguese and Spanish began to produce sugar, wealthy families could afford it, but it was so costly that they bought it by the ounce.

In England, during the sixteenth century when sugar had become cheaper, the Elizabethans seemed almost to be made of sugar and spice. They carried around with them little boxes of comfits and suckets, sweet candies made of everything from orange pips to green walnuts, double-dipped in boiling syrup. Queen Elizabeth I even popped comfits into her mouth during meetings of her Privy Council.

Besides candy, the Elizabethans ate a variety of cakes—soft saffron cake; flans (open fruit tarts); sweet bread; and puff pastries made with flour, cream, and plenty of sugar.

By the early nineteenth century, sugar was a staple on the grocery shelf. It revolutionized cake-making. Everywhere, bakers got highly satisfying results with the new ingredient. When baking powder and compressed yeast were invented, there was simply no end to the cakes that could be made.

In France, the *pâtisseurs* (pastrycooks) set up tables where their patrons could drool over éclairs, meringues, and *petits fours,* those "little somethings from the oven," covered with icing and fantastically shaped and decorated. Today, as then, the *pâtisseries,* or pastry shops, of France are well patronized.

In Austria, bakers shuddered at the very idea of baking their new masterpieces in·an ordinary oven, so they set up special ovens for cake-baking. In 1832, Viennese master chef Edouard

Sacher, owner of the Hotel Sacher, invented mouth-watering *tortes,* rich cakes made with very little flour but with lots of ground nuts, jam, and chocolate. His *Sachertorte,* consisting of many layers of chocolate cake iced with still more chocolate and put together with jam, became world famous.

For years, people argued about who made the original *Sachertorte.* Was it Edouard Sacher? Or was it Demel, another Viennese pastry cook? Demel's *torte* was excellent, but he used no jam. After seven years, a judge ruled that Edouard Sacher had made the original *Sachertorte,* but cake-lovers are still arguing about which is the better *torte.*

The chocolate that Edouard Sacher used so lavishly became a highly popular ingredient for cakes. A true product of the New World, it was, like sugar, a long time coming. Hernando Cortez, the Spanish explorer, learned about *chocolatl,* as it was called, from the Aztec Indians of Mexico in the early sixteenth century. Unsweetened and flavored with spices, it was a drink rather than a food. The Aztec emperors liked huge quantities of it. They called it the food of the gods and drank it ceremoniously from golden goblets.

The Spaniards took chocolate back with them to Europe, where it was warmly welcomed in Spain, Italy, France, Great Britain, and other countries. Cane sugar was added to sweeten it. In England, a Londoner described it in his diary as "a very hearty drink." People gave chocolate parties in their homes, and chocolate houses opened where men dropped in to play chess, pick up their mail, leave messages for their friends and, of course, drink chocolate. Fashionable ladies would have their maids bring them steaming cups of chocolate in church, so that they could sip it luxuriously during the sermon.

Chocolate was not used for eating and cooking until the early nineteenth century, when some unknown person got the idea of adding cocoa butter to milk chocolate powder and making blocks of eating chocolate. In Switzerland, Daniel Peter shaped his chocolate into sweet, firm bars, and no mountaineer would dream of climbing in the Alps without a supply of Peter's Milk Chocolate in his knapsack.

In America, the colonists of New England first heard about drinking chocolate in letters from their English friends. Trading vessels began to bring supplies of chocolate. Colonial families thought it delicious, but it was so expensive that for years it was considered a special treat.

Then, some years before the American Revolution, a man named James Baker helped a poor immigrant open a small chocolate mill on the bank of the Neponset River in Massachusetts. Other mills followed. Chocolate became cheaper, and both drinking and eating chocolate began to be made in America. It was produced in solid, liquid, and powder forms. Of the two basic kinds of solid chocolate, American chocolate now seems to be better for cooking, and English chocolate better for eating.

Chocolate cookery is highly popular in America, where we enjoy a great variety of chocolate cakes, cookies, pies, and other desserts. This is because Americans are fortunate enough to have the right kind of chocolate for every purpose (unsweetened, semisweet, semiliquid, bits, chips, pieces, etc.), for only the right kind of chocolate will give perfect results.

four
Fit for a Feast Day

Of all the cakes we eat, the ceremonial cakes are the oldest. From the beginning of Christianity, the faithful served feast day cakes as a reminder of God's bounty and of the Christian virtue of charity. God cakes, triangular in shape to symbolize the Father, Son, and Holy Ghost, are still eaten in England, and the recipe has recently been adapted to American taste.

Christmas, New Year, Easter, and Halloween had their special cakes. On New Year's Day, English youngsters who visited their godparents and asked for a blessing were given a bonus, a God cake stuffed with currants and spices.

During Lent, from Ash Wednesday to Easter Sunday, with a few exceptions, cake was given up. The Russians, Serbs, and Greeks, once the strictest of Lent-keepers, did not eat a crumb of cake until mid-Lent Sunday. Then they broke their fast with sweet little cakes, shaped like crosses. The English broke theirs with simnel cakes (see pp. 66-67), little fruitcakes topped with

27

marzipan, still an Easter treat today. These date back to the Middle Ages, and the custom of "mothering." Boys and girls who worked away from home were allowed a holiday on mid-Lent Sunday to visit their home church and their mothers. They brought Mother simnel cake and flowers and, as a special treat, did all her housework on that Sunday.

On Good Friday the peoples of many countries ate buns baked with a cross marked on them to symbolize the cross of Christ. This custom may have started in Saint Alban's Abbey in England in 1361 when the monks distributed these hot cross buns to the poor. The special buns became a famous Good Friday feature in England, Ireland, and later in America. They were made of spiced dough, round in shape, and the cross was made of icing. In England, two royal bun houses in the Chelsea district of London turned them out by the thousands on Good Friday morning.

Long ago, they were also sold by street peddlers, who sang such ditties as this:

> Hot cross buns, hot cross buns,
> One a penny, two a penny,
> Hot cross buns.
>
> If your daughters won't eat them,
> Give them to your sons;
> But if you have none of those little elves
> Then you must eat them all yourselves.

On Holy Saturday there was great activity around the house, especially in central Europe. Eggs were boiled and painted, Easter ham and other foods were cooked, and Easter bread and pastry were baked. In Russia, it was the custom after midnight to bless the *paska,* or Easter bread. This was really a small cake, flavored with saffron and made in a pyramid shape. It was carried to the priest to be blessed and then brought home and given a place of honor on the Easter breakfast table.

Cake was a highlight of the Easter celebrations in Greece and Russia. It used to be taken to church on Easter Sunday to be blessed with the family. Catholics in America are now reviving the symbolic lamb cake, which they serve as an Easter dessert. Author Mary Reed Newland, who has seven cake-loving children, makes her own pattern. She cuts a large, flat, oblong cake into the shape of a lamb and ices it with coconut frosting to give it a woolly look.

On the religious feast of All Hallows' Eve (from which Halloween takes its name, although it is not a religious feast) many Europeans nibble at bones of the dead, beans of the dead, and soul cakes. Bones are special little pastries, doled out to the poor in northern Spain and in Madrid. Beans are rich and delicious little almond cakes that are eaten by Italians when they come home from decorating the family graves. Soul cakes were given to beggars in England—if they promised to pray for the dead of the household.

A story goes that a pious cook, determined that the beggar should be reminded of eternity with every bite he took, made a hole in a soul cake to symbolize life everlasting, dropped it into bubbling fat—and invented the doughnut!

In all Christian countries, Christmas was celebrated (and, to some extent, is still celebrated) with many kinds of cake. In most countries, the cakes baked on Christmas Eve and eaten during Christmas week were supposed to bring special blessings of good luck and health. In Ireland, England, and Scotland, a cake was baked on Christmas Eve for every member of the family. They were usually little round cakes, flavored with caraway seeds. If anyone's cake happened to break as it came from the oven, it was supposed to be an omen of bad luck. The Irish have a Gaelic name for Christmas Eve—*Oidhche na Ceapairi*—which means "night of cakes."

The Christmas cakes were decorated differently in different countries. German and French cooks liked to adorn them with a little figure of the Christ Child, made of sugar. Greek Christmas cakes had a cross on the top, and one of the cakes was left on the table during Holy Night in the hope that Christ himself would come to eat it. A Christmas loaf, called *Pain Calendeau,* is still made in southern France, but it must not be eaten until the first quarter has been given to some poor person.

Besides their Christmas loaves, the Slavic nations bake thin wafers of white flour, which they eat with syrup or honey before the main meal on Christmas Eve. The Lithuanians call them "bread of the angels." Scenes of the Nativity are imprinted on them, and the father of the family distributes them as a symbol of peace and love. In Russia, Saint Nicholas, or *Kolya,* is said to put wheat cakes on the windowsill during Holy Night, but, though the cakes are there, no one has yet caught him at it.

While many of the ancient cakes have disappeared, dozens of other Christmas pastries, cookies, and cakes have been substituted for them. In Germany, Austria, Switzerland, and other parts of Europe, the children wait eagerly for the *Weinachtsgebäck,* or Christmas tree pastry, to make its appearance. Made of white dough and cut into the shapes of angels, stars, flowers, and animals, it is hung on the Christmas tree and eaten by the children when the tree is taken down. *Honigbackwerk,* or honey pastry, made of flour, honey, ginger and other spices, is a favorite Christmas dish all over Germany. Other varieties, very hard and crunchy, are the south German *Springerle,* rectangular in shape with pictures stamped on them—flowers, animals, dancing figures, and Christmas symbols.

There are many other Christmas cakes and cake customs, but

perhaps the most delightful is a custom still practiced in parts of England and France. This is the baking of the King's Cake, on Epiphany Day, January 6, in honor of the Magi, the wise men who brought gifts to the newborn Christ. A coin is put into the dough before it is baked, and the person who finds it in his slice is the "king." In French Canada this cake, called *gâteau des rois* (cake of the kings) contains a bean and a pea. The finders are "king" and "queen" of the feast.

Besides the cakes baked for religious occasions, there were also saints' cakes to honor special saints. Some of these got their names from their shape. St. Joseph's Fingers, a favorite in Sicily, were shared with the poor on his feast day.

In Poland, when the first snow fell, children cried out, "St. Martin comes riding on his white horse!" This was the signal for mothers to set about making St. Martin's Horseshoes, rich little almond cakes shaped like horseshoes. Just as St. Martin shared his cloak with a beggar, so grownups had to share their horseshoes with the hordes of youngsters who came begging on his feast day.

On St. Catherine's feast day, English spinsters and lace-makers ate St. Catherine's Wigs, so called because the batter, baked in round pans, curled over the edge like the curls of a wig. Spinsters, eating their wigs, would implore their patroness to send them a husband.

With dozens of foreign cookbooks in the bookstores today, American families can enjoy cakes that have long been popular in the lands of their forebears.

five
Birthday Cake, with Candles

A mother dropped into her neighborhood bakery one day to order a big, pink birthday cake. She wanted special decorations to be put on it. "Leave enough space for candles," she said, "twenty-one this time!" A sudden thought made her eyes widen. "What a mountain of birthday cake I must have bought for my children," she said. "I wonder how it all started? Birthday cakes, I mean."

The bakery clerk hadn't a clue. Nevertheless, we can find many clues in history. Men and women have been celebrating their birthdays ever since the calendar was invented, and cake was an early feature of the festivities. A letter written by the Roman emperor Hadrian tells of the banquet that was being prepared for his birthday. There were to be cakes in abundance. The emperor was so sorry for those who were unable to accept his invitation that he ordered the royal baker to make extra cakes and have them sent by messenger to the absentees.

33

The ancient Persians were contemptuous of Greek feasts because the Greeks seldom served any dessert except fruits and honey. The Persians were very lavish, especially at birthday celebrations. Long trestle tables were set up in the gardens. An ox, a camel, and a donkey were roasted over great fires, and the meat course was followed by a dessert of pastries and cake. Persian bakers excelled at making many kinds of small, sweet cakes.

The first birthday described in the Bible is that of the pharaoh who was king of Egypt about four thousand years ago. He not only gave a splendid feast for his guests but also invited his servants and slaves. The king even ordered the prisoners in the royal jail to be set free to join the celebration.

In ancient Rome, only the birthday of the emperor was celebrated, but the common people still had their cake. A man called Fulvius, a wealthy wool spinner, used to honor the emperor's birthday by providing free cake for all the inhabitants of the city.

During the Dark Ages, when the Roman Empire declined in power and splendor, birthday celebrations disappeared, and birthday cakes with them. Except in the case of royal children, no birth records were kept. Commoners did not know when they were born and had only a vague idea of how old they were. Christians in those days did not even celebrate the birth of Christ, because they believed that birthday feasts were pagan and sinful.

Though many of the nobles ignored the church's ruling and continued to hold birthday celebrations, no mention was made of birthday cakes. They did not return until the twelfth century when children, who were always named after a saint or holy person, celebrated their name day, or saint's day, rather than their birthday. For many years, the name day continued to be more important than the birthday. "Any calf can have a birthday, but only a Christian can have a name day,'' the peasants used to say. The children were taught the history and legend of their own saint, who was believed to be their special protector as long as they lived.

The name day was a joyful feast day for the whole family. Usually, the name day child began his day by going to church. On his return the whole family congratulated him, offering good wishes and little gifts. Then everyone sat down to a festive breakfast at a gaily decorated table. The one whose feast day was being celebrated had a holiday, with freedom from household or farming chores.

The favorite cake for the name day, still baked in many European countries, was a luscious concoction, rich in cream, butter, raisins, and almonds. It was baked in a fluted tube pan. It is called *Napfkuchen* in Germany, *Gugelhupf* in Austria, *Kuglof* in Hungary, and *Babka* among the Slavic nations.

Birthday cakes today come in all shapes and sizes. Many of the iced and decorated cakes are square or round. The square shapes are supposed to be related to Egyptian architecture. The round ones are inspired by Greek architects, who liked to use cylindrical shapes.

You can have extra fun on your birthday by letting your cake tell fortunes. For this purpose a coin, a button, a ring, and a thimble are put into the dough before the cake is baked. When it is sliced, anyone who gets one of these objects in a slice can tell what his or her future is going to be. The one who gets the coin will be wealthy, but the one with the button will be poor. The person who gets the ring will be married, but the one who gets the thimble will remain single.

The custom of decorating the birthday cake with lighted candles is thought to have been started by the Germans. They probably adopted an old belief of the Greeks and Romans—that lighted tapers and candles had magical qualities. These early people used to light fires on the altars of their gods as a sign of honor and respect. They believed their prayers would waft upwards on the flames and the gods, in return, would shower blessings upon them. On the birthday of Artemis, goddess of the moon and the hunt, honey cakes "round as the moon and lit with tapers" were placed on the temple altars of the goddess.

Centuries later, in German birthday celebrations, a large candle known as the *Lebenslicht,* or light of life, was set in the middle of the birthday cake and surrounded by as many candles as the birthday child had years. It was considered unlucky if anyone except the birthday child blew out the light of life. If a wish was made when the child blew out the candle flame, the wish was supposed to come true in as many months as it took puffs. If those persons celebrating their birthdays were very old, they had to be satisfied with a single candle.

In some parts of Germany, birthdays were celebrated in a different way. A little fir tree, similar to the one used at Christmas, was set up on a white-covered table. It was decorated with gilded walnuts and almonds and surrounded by the birthday gifts. There was a long cake, ablaze with lighted candles. The guest of honor blew them out, and the number of puffs this took represented the number of years that would pass before he or she got married.

The cake, filled with fruits and nuts and thickly powdered with white sugar, was called *Stollen.* It was shaped like the oblong cake served at Christmas and intended to look like the Christ Child in swaddling clothes. At Christmas, we still find *Stollen* on sale in Germany and in American bakeries.

This custom was carried to England by German visitors who happened to be there on their birthdays. From England, it found its way to America, where it sometimes changed its shape.

In Italy, although a birthday cake was served, the most important feature of the festivities was a torch march in which relatives and friends honored the birthday child. Wealthy families carried wax tapers, while the poor used wooden torches. The number of lights corresponded with the age of the birthday child. After the procession, the torches were used to light the birthday cake. When electric lights became common, Italians placed small candles on the cake and lit them as a reminder of the old torchlight procession.

An American bakery made the world's biggest birthday cake. This was trucked to the nation's birthplace, Philadelphia, and was displayed in Memorial Hall on July 3, 1976, in honor of America's Bicentennial.

Over fifty-five thousand people gaped at the huge and handsome cake. Fifty feet high, and forty-two feet wide at its base, it required ten thousand man-hours to bake, decorate, and assemble and weighed forty thousand pounds. Made from a basic chocolate cake recipe and iced with butter cream, it was decorated with large murals, showing highlights of American history, from the Declaration of Independence to the moon walk.

Because it would not have been practical to slice the great cake while long lines of people waited, the onlookers were served cupcakes made of the same ingredients as the Bicentennial cake. The next day large sections of the cake were given to hospitals and orphanages. The frosting paintings were returned to the bakery where they were treated with transparent plastic to make them permanent. Many are now in museums and historical societies throughout the country.

six
Love's Old, Sweet Cake

The professional baker exercises his greatest skill on his wedding cakes, especially in their decorations. Usually the cake is shaped like a pyramid, but it can take any form the bridal pair wishes.

Often the cake is topped with a sugary bridal couple sailing off on the voyage of life in a catboat loaded with orange blossoms. Sometimes a plump cupid beams from the cake, or Hymen, the god of marriage, is posed on the top, dressed like a ballet dancer of half a century ago. Usually, however, a standing figure of the bride and groom is the favorite decoration.

German bakeshops offer their customers all kinds of sweet and sentimental ornaments. Most popular is a loving pair of little starch figures, standing beneath a bunch of orange blossoms as if they were just pronouncing their marriage vows.

Whether the cake is large and imposing or small and simple, the bride usually likes to keep a portion of it a long time. For generations, couples used to preserve the top part of the cake to serve at the christening party of their first child. Some even store a large portion of the cake to be brought out on their twenty-fifth wedding anniversary!

The custom of using bread, which preceded cake in wedding ceremonies, goes back to ancient times. Some kind of bread custom is known all over the world. The earliest pagans danced around a heap of burning corn during marriage ceremonies. The twentieth-century savage squats on a loaf of bread during the wedding ceremony, or the groom twines a lock of his hair with a lock of the bride's, using a wisp of rice straw.

The wedding cake, rather than bread, first appeared among the wealthy nobles of ancient Rome. The cake was crumbled over the bride's head as a sign of plentifulness, and the guests took some cake to make sure of plentifulness for themselves.

In Britain, the Anglo-Saxons had huge baskets of small, dry crackers at their marriage ceremonies. Each guest took a cracker home. The remaining crackers were given to the poor. After a time, people began to want something more tasty than these unappetizing biscuits so, in the time of Queen Elizabeth I, small currant cakes made with eggs, butter, sugar, and spice became fashionable. It was not long before an imaginative baker began to top these cakes with almond paste.

The next step was to substitute one large cake for the collection of small ones. This was supposed to be the idea of a brilliant French cook. While traveling in England, he decided that the custom of piling up a lot of small cakes was inconvenient, so he mashed them together into a mound, and iced the mound. Thus the first wedding cake was born. True to the old custom, the cake was still broken over the bride's head. But, gradually, this practice was discontinued, and the cake was cut into pieces and given to the guests the way we do today.

Sometimes the wedding cake was very large. John Sykes, describing a wedding in the little town of Bishopswearmouth, England, on May 21, 1753, says that "the bride's pie was carried between two persons on a hand-barrow to the bake-house." In Hungary, too, the wedding cake was often huge and was thickly covered with ornaments. In some parts of the country, small cakes shaped like churches, stags, cocks, and so on were brought by guests as gifts for the bride. Sometimes curiously fashioned cakes were tossed in the air for guests to catch.

Many superstitions were connected with the wedding cake. In Britain, before the single cake came into use, the bride and groom tried to kiss each other over the huge pile of small spice cakes given by the guests. If they succeeded, they were supposed to be sure of lifelong prosperity.

It was, and still is, the right of the bride to cut the first slice of the cake. If anyone else does it, he or she "cuts into the happiness and prosperity of the bride."

In some parts of England there was an important ceremony of passing small portions of the wedding cake through the wedding ring. This had to be done very precisely. The bride held the ring between the finger and thumb of her right hand, and the groom pushed the piece of cake through the ring nine times. The bits of cake were then given to the guests as charms. If a maiden placed the charm in the foot of her left stocking and put it under her pillow before going to bed, it was believed that she would surely dream of the man she was to marry.

In Burnley, England, a wedding ring and a sixpence were put into an ordinary flat currant cake. Just before the guests left, the cake was broken and given to the single women. The one who found the ring in her portion would shortly be married, but the one who found the sixpence would die an old maid.

seven
The Super-Cakes:
Cheesecake and Gingerbread

Cheesecake and gingerbread have been popular for so long that they deserve a chapter to themselves. Cheesecake goes as far back as the written language, but nobody knows when gingerbread was first made.

It is not surprising that pictures of starlets in pretty poses are slangily called cheesecake, since cheesecake has plenty of eye appeal. It is often prettified with whirls of whipped cream or sour cream, glazed with apricot or strawberry, or decorated with chocolate curls, tiny bits of citron or angelica, or currants steeped in wine.

The ancient Greeks thought highly of cheesecake. They wrote learned treatises, songs, and poems in praise of it and offered it to their gods. In early Greece a village was named Cheesecake.

Socrates, the great Greek philosopher, could not resist cheesecake, although otherwise he ate sparingly and did not care for food or drink. His friends often brought him cheesecake, to

42

the annoyance of his bad-tempered wife, Xanthippe. On one occasion, she grabbed her husband's cheesecake, threw it on to the floor, and trampled it to bits. The peaceable Socrates only smiled, "Ah well," he said, "you won't get any of it yourself."

Cheesecake was always served at Greek weddings, where the bridegroom made his bride a gift of the cake. Other cakes were roasted on hot coals and given to the bridegroom's friends with large servings of honey.

That other early favorite, gingerbread, was relished by the Romans. Pliny, a Roman writer, tells how gingerbread was offered at banquets, together with such delicacies as pigs' livers and the tongues of flamingoes.

The atmosphere has a great effect on gingerbread. The slightest moisture in the air causes the cake to soften, while dry weather makes it harden. The practical Germans made an excellent barometer out of it. They baked a gingerbread cake in the shape of a general and hung it in the entrance hall of the house. When the master left home in the morning, he would ask the servant, "What does the general say?" If the gingerbread was soft, he knew he needed to take his umbrella. If it was dry, he could expect a fine day.

The gingerbread recipe was brought to the New World on the *Mayflower.* It was one of the first cakes baked in New England. A special kind, called Muster Gingerbread, is still made in honor of a New England tradition.

Before the Civil War, the first Tuesday of every June was set aside as Muster Day. On that day, the men eighteen to forty-five assembled for military training. At nine o'clock in the morning, companies of militia gathered on the village parade ground to drill and march. Their families came in crowds to watch them. When the parades were over, everyone had an appetite and ate huge quantities of gingerbread. The most popular kind was baked in a thin sheet and cut into slabs. It is still an American favorite, especially in New England, where it is now known as Old Buttermilk Gingerbread.

Centuries earlier, the English began to bake gingerbread. No one knows where they learned about it or how they got the recipe. It was probably first made by monks in the old monasteries, and by that time had become very delicious. Fit for a king, it was served at royal tables even before the days of William the Conqueror, an English king who came to the throne on Christmas Day, 1066.

In the eighteenth century, gingerbread sellers mingled with street vendors and workers who cried their wares or their callings in the streets of London. The cries varied from "Who'll buy my lavender?" to "I cash clo' " (Meaning "I pay cash for your old clothes"). The most spectacular of street vendors was Ford, the gingerbread man, who was usually known as Tiddy Doll from a song he used to sing. He wore a white-ruffled shirt, a lace trimmed hat, and a very fine apron. Not only was Tiddy Doll magnificent to look at, but his melodious singing voice brought Londoners running to buy his wares.

A general fondness for gingerbread spread as far as the East Indies. All countries enjoyed and baked it according to their own ideas. Gingerbread was made and sold in Paris as early as the fourteenth century. In France a Gingerbread Fair was held at Easter time. In Holland, people guarded their recipes jealously and handed them down from parent to child.

England, too, has a traditional gingerbread that, for some reason, is called parkin. It first appeared on Guy Fawkes Day. Guy Fawkes, a man of cool daring, was asked to join a conspiracy to blow up the Houses of Parliament and King James I when he came to open Parliament on November 5, 1605.

The conspirators worked boldly. In May of that year, they

managed to get possession of a vault under the Houses of Parliament and stored thirty-six barrels of gunpowder. While they were making their plans to set off the gunpowder, an anonymous letter was sent to one of the members of Parliament. A search was made in the cellars, the gunpowder was discovered, and Guy Fawkes was arrested and later executed. England still celebrates his day with bonfires, fireworks, and effigies called "guys." Parkin, a coarse-textured gingerbread made with rolled oats, is baked specially for the occasion and is eaten with butter, or topped with whipped cream.

Today, every cookbook has its own recipes for gingerbread. In *The Joy of Cooking,* Irma S. Rombauer tells not only how to make gingerbread cake but how to shape and bake a gingerbread house and perky little gingerbread men.

eight
Cakes in the New World

Although America was to have many elaborate cake recipes, her first cakes were as simple as those in the Bible. When the Pilgrims landed on the rocky shores of Massachusetts, they rejoiced to find cornfields abandoned by Indians, with grain ready for harvesting. They were also visited by friendly tribes, who brought them cornmeal and taught them how to make ashcakes.

These tasted better than they sound and were enjoyed for many years. In 1938, a cook found a three-hundred-year-old recipe for ashcakes and baked some for her family. "Add a Teaspoonful of Salt to a Quart of sifted Corn Meal. Make up with boiling Water and knead well. Make into round, flat Cakes. Sweep a clean Place on the hottest Part of the Hearth. Put the Cake on it and cover it with hot Wood Ashes. Wash and wipe it dry before eating it. Sometimes a Cabbage Leaf is placed under it, and one over it, before baking, in which Case it need not be washed."

When wives promised their husbands that there would be ashcakes for supper, they came home from work in good time. The cakes tasted better when hot from the oven and were well soaked in butter.

By the eighteenth century, many kinds of cake were being made, especially in the great houses of plantation owners in Virginia and Maryland. Martha Custis, George Washington's wife, baked a great cake that must have been big enough for a banquet although she described it simply as "for my grandmama." The recipe was found in an old manuscript, dated Mt. Vernon, 1781.

"Take forty eggs," says Martha's recipe, "and divide the whites from the yolks and beat them to a froth.

"Then work four pounds of butter to a cream, and put the whites of the eggs to it, a tablespoonful at a time, until it is well worked.

"Then put four pounds of sugar, well powdered, to it in the same manner.

"Then put in the yolks of eggs and five pounds of flour and five pounds of fruit.

"Two hours will bake it."

For over 150 years, the colonists had to use their own recipes. Then cookbooks began to be written; some 740 appeared in 120 years. Among them was one compiled by Amelia Simmons, a young woman who was very knowledgeable about cakes. Her book included recipes for "all kinds of cakes, from the Imperial Plumb to the Plain Cake, adopted in this country in all grades of life." Amelia, an orphan herself, advised other orphans to learn to cook and bake, so that they would be welcome everywhere "and even attract husbands."

In Maryland, cake had to compete with something that was not quite cake, not quite bread, and not quite cooky—the Maryland beaten biscuit, which was made with shortening but without sugar. An old gentleman told author Katherine Anne Smallzreid that the dough "should be beaten with the flat side of an axe until it raises little blisters and is smooth and satiny." Another beaten biscuit lover, Howard Weeden, author of *Bandanna Ballads,* tells her own secret.

> Two hundred licks is what I gives
> For home-folks, never fewer,
> An' if I'm 'specting company in,
> I gives five hundred sure!

Between 1620 and 1670, Dutch colonists settled in New England but were soon ousted by the British. They gave us one of our favorite recipes—the *oly koeck,* or doughnut. These were served at christening parties, together with *krullers* (crullers) and a hot, lemony drink called *caudle.* By 1898, the *oly koeck* had changed its shape, and Mrs. Van Rensseler, who wrote a lively book about the Dutch housewife, complained bitterly that the modern doughnut was "a base imitation." The real one, she insisted, always had a nut or a raisin in the center.

In the nineteenth century, when a new wave of Dutch immigrants came to settle in Michigan, they brought with them the recipe for at least one delicious cake—Dutch Apple. This consists of apple slices, sprinkled with sugar and cinnamon, poured into the bottom of a pan and topped with one-egg cake batter. To make it even sweeter, it was served with brown sugar sauce.

German immigrants who settled in Pennsylvania and New York, as well as those who later moved to the western states, opened the first bakeries where cookies and coffee cakes were baked and sold. Unfortunately, German cookery was mistakenly called Pennsylvania Dutch—and the name stuck. This happened because when the Germans explained that they spoke *Deutsch* (German), their Quaker neighbors thought that the word meant "Dutch."

nine
Enter the Layer Cake

Americans had developed such a sweet tooth by the beginning of the nineteenth century that *Practical Housekeeping* alone told how to make 128 different cakes. The ingredients were easy to get.

Sugar had greatly improved since Columbus took the cane to the West Indies. In colonial times it had been pressed into a stone-hard cake and hung on a hook from the pantry ceiling. When needed, the housewife had to hack off a portion with her sugar scissors and grind it in a mortar with a hand pestle. This tiresome process continued until 1794, when a New Orleans man, Etienne de Bors, invented a way of granulating sugar.

Up to this time, there had been no special flour for making cakes. Americans had continued to use cornmeal, in spite of the strong protests of the "casket girls" early in the eighteenth century.

These young women had been sent from reform schools in

France to New Orleans, where the settlers were saying that they needed wives. In 1777, a boatload of girls arrived, chaperoned by nuns with whom they lived until they were married. The French government provided each girl with a casket containing caps, chemises, and underwear.

Living conditions were hard in New Orleans, but the casket girls made the best of their new surroundings. They put up with houses that were little better than shacks and cheerfully lifted their skirts when crossing muddy roads. But they complained long and loud about having to eat cornmeal three times a day and begged for the good white flour of France.

They did not get their fine white flour. Instead, they were taught how to make the best use of the plentiful cornmeal. Wheat flour appeared much later, when settlers moved west and found the right kind of land for growing wheat.

When wheat flour came it was a big improvement, but there was something even better in store for cake bakers. In Evansville, Indiana, in 1856, a young man named Addison Iglehart wondered why some kinds of flour made better cakes than others. He began to experiment with winter wheat, using only the most tender part. He ground it, sifted it through a silk screen, and ground it again. The result was a flour so light and airy that it became known as a cake flour.

Baking powder, another great help for the cook, also appeared in the late nineteenth century, but nobody knows who invented it. Bakers found it a great boon; it saved them hours of beating. With cake flour and baking powder at hand, America soon devised a cake of her own—the layer cake. Both chocolate and coconut layer cakes became highly popular. Chocolate, made from the cacao bean, was native to the New World and easy to use for cooking.

Coconut was easy to import from Cuba and the West Indies, but it was difficult to prepare. According to *Practical Housekeeping,* the cook had to "cut a hole through the meat at one of the holes in the end, draw off the milk, pound the nut well on all sides to loosen the meat, crack, take out the meat, and set the pieces in a heater or in a cool, open oven over night, or for a few hours, to dry, then grate; if all is not used, sprinkle with sugar (after grating) and spread out in a cool, dry place, and it will keep for weeks."

Few cooks wanted to go to that much trouble, so they made more chocolate layer cakes than coconut—until 1895. In that year, grated coconut came into being as a result of a business failure. A Philadelphia flour miller, Franklin Baker, sold a large quantity of his flour to a customer in Cuba. The customer wrote to him, saying that a revolution had broken out and that he could not pay cash for the flour. Instead of money he sent a cargo of coconuts.

Franklin Baker looked gloomily at his large supply of coconuts. What use were they to a flour miller? He decided to sell them, but he found only one coconut dealer—a man who told him disgustedly that he was about to go out of business. Instead of selling his own coconuts, Franklin added to them by buying the dealer's stock at a bargain price.

Knowing that he would have trouble selling the coconuts in their natural state, he looked around the country for machinery that would shred and package them. Before long, he found a suitable machine and put it to work. The grated, packaged coconut sold readily. At the end of two years, Franklin gave up his flour mill and devoted all his time to selling coconut.

The coconut layer cake, now simple to make, caught up in popularity with that other favorite, the chocolate layer.

ten
From Angel to Devil

Centuries ago, sponge cake was known as Savoy cake, a name it still has in Europe.

At one time, the counts of Savoy possessed wide dominions on the borders of Italy and Burgundy. In the thirteenth century, four of the beautiful daughters of Berthe of Savoy married into royal families. Each girl took the family sponge cake recipe with her, and its fame spread widely. One daughter lived in a mansion on the banks of the River Thames in London. In her honor, the great house was given the name Savoy. On the same spot, today, stands a famous hotel, the Savoy Hotel. Every day, great sheets of Savoy cake are baked in its kitchens to be used by the pastry chef as a basis for a number of mouth-watering desserts.

Sponge cake was an early favorite in America, where most people found it quite good in its original form. Others, however, decided that the cake needed fillings or toppings or icings to enhance its flavor, so in time, many varieties of sponge cake were baked in American kitchens.

54

One of the most popular is jelly roll. This consists of a sheet of batter, baked for a short time at a very high temperature to keep it flexible. While still warm, it is thickly spread with jelly or jam and rolled up into a log. Some cooks fill it with chocolate, cream, fruit, or whatever they fancy.

Chiffon cake, another variety of sponge cake, was invented by an insurance salesman in 1927. He managed to keep the recipe a secret for twenty years. In 1947, when he presented his mystery formula to the public, it was discovered that the secret ingredient was the addition of salad or cooking oil to the sponge cake batter. This liquid shortening, when used in just the right proportion and blended by a new method, resulted in a uniquely rich and delicate cake. If you buy chiffon cake at a bakery today, you will probably find many flavors to choose from—orange, maple nut, spice, lemon, and chocolate.

Two people, a woman and a man, claim to have invented angel cake, or angel food cake. According to one story, a family living in an Atlantic coast city moved to a picturesque spot on the Hudson River in New York. There they opened a boarding house, and one of the ladies of the family became known for her tempting cakes. A friend gave her a recipe that had come to her from India. When the family returned home, she began to bake the cake for sale. As she did not want the recipe to be known (which would reduce her sales), she baked the cake in secret. But in spite of her precautions, the secret eventually leaked out, and other cooks began to make angel cake, improving it and sending the recipe to distant friends until it won a national reputation.

The second story says that angel cake originated in St. Louis, Missouri, about 1890. A restaurant owner named Sides featured it in his elegant dining room. The cake became so famous that it was baked to order and even shipped to customers living abroad. Mr. Sides did his best to keep the recipe to himself, telling everyone that a special kind of powder was needed for it and that he alone knew where to get it. Curious bakers and chefs soon discovered that the mysterious powder was cream of tartar, a substance used in medicines which could be bought in any drugstore. Before long, cake-lovers who wanted angel cake could make their own.

Although cooks have been making chocolate cakes for over two hundred years, devil's food cake is a modern name for very chocolaty cake, usually a layer cake, iced and put together with white icing.

The name probably first appeared in one of those little cookbooks that women's clubs put out to raise funds, but there is no way of proving this. Certainly the cake was known before 1902, when the Walter Baker Company put out a recipe for Spanish chocolate cake, made precisely in the same way as devil's food cake. This leads some cooks to believe that the name "devil's food" was not invented in America but came to us from sunny Spain.

eleven
More American Cakes

American bakers still enjoy a variety of cakes from the Old World, but they have invented many others that use ingredients that are typically American. Little pumpkin tarts, scalloped and sprinkled with chopped nuts, are made in many states. Molasses has made possible the Creole Ginger Cake of New Orleans, and the Old, Old Molasses Cake of Virginia.

Pennsylvania has developed a great number of breakfast cakes, most of them with crumb toppings. Few recipes for sweet crumbs appear in old handwritten cookbooks. They were not needed; the Pennsylvania housewife baked so many crumb cakes that she could almost make them in her sleep.

Southern cake is very rich. Robert E. Lee Cake, one of the most famous historical cakes, uses ten eggs. Miss Mollie Pryor's White Pound Cake calls for sixteen egg whites! Another Southern dessert has such a super-rich filling that it has become known as Utterly Deadly Southern Pecan Pie.

Some cake recipes are guarded as heirlooms. Chinese Mooncake, for instance, is traditionally eaten by Chinese-Americans on the fifteenth day of the eighth moon, when as many foods as possible are made in a round shape. Cookbook author Dorothy Spicer tried to get the recipe to put in her new cookbook. But she was told that "old people make the cake from memory, and they are quite unwilling to reveal the secret—even to inquiring daughters."

In Paradise Valley of Arizona, a lady used to come to every baking contest with the same delicious cake. The recipe was the property of her cook, who refused to part with it for less than a hundred dollars. In her *Missouri Traveler Cookbook,* Mary Horsford gives the recipe for Hundred Dollar Cake.

The recipe for Queen Elizabeth's cake, the one she prefers to all others, is hard to get, but Mary Horsford gives that one too. She tells how an American garden club, touring England, managed to get the recipe from Buckingham Palace, where the queen lives. They brought it home and sold hundreds of copies for charity.

Recently, America has decided that cake-baking is a highly distinguished craft and that some of our elaborate cakes should be museum pieces. In October, 1976, the Museum of Contemporary Crafts in New York City opened a cake display.

Instead of saying PLEASE DO NOT TOUCH, the signs warned PLEASE DO NOT EAT. (In case visitors could not resist nibbling, the museum kept jars of jelly beans and candy corn at hand.) Many of the cakes were edible, or partly edible, but some were models made of styrofoam, wool, polyester, and other materials.

A cake artist from New Haven, Connecticut, showed a styrofoam cake with hard icing that looked like needlepoint and was decorated with fifteen thousand stars. One cook brought a towering cake, dripping with chocolate drops, jelly beans, and candy corn. Another submitted a cake that had a replica of King Kong climbing out of its top.

Paul Smith, the museum director, said he was sure that this was the first time a museum had had a show of cakes. "And I'm certain that this show will inspire artistry in cake-bakers," he continued. "And next time someone bakes a birthday cake, instead of the usual shape with rosebuds and candles, maybe he or she will try something different."

twelve
The Magical Cake Mix

Wonderful things continue to happen to cake. Perhaps the most exciting is the recent invention of cake mixes. These did not come along until about the middle of the present century, but their story really began in 1864. At that time a clever chemist, experimenting in his laboratory, discovered baking powder. Flour millers used it as an important ingredient in self-rising flour and pancake mix.

About 1920, a doughnut mix was made. It was warmly welcomed, especially since an automatic doughnut machine came on the market at the same time.

Between the two world wars, packages of cake mix began to appear on grocery shelves. Housewives were not very enthusiastic about them, however, and only lazy or curious cooks tried them. Good cooks simply could not believe that a cake made from a mix could be as good as one they made themselves from scratch. When World War II caused a shortage of sugar and other

ingredients, however, women turned hopefully to cake mixes
and found them surprisingly good.

The story of cake mixes is a story of challenge. In 1943 several
big research kitchens competed with one another to make
acceptable devil's food, spice, and white cake mixes. Tests and
more tests were made, and recipe after recipe was tried in
attempts to find the best one for each kind of cake. The problem
was to put together a mix that could be mass-produced and
would keep its flavor and quality for long periods in grocery
stores.

Every ingredient was important, and progress was slow. It took
several months just to find the right type of shortening, one that
would stay fresh and sweet for a long time.

The package, too, had to be carefully considered. It had to be
sturdy, greaseproof, and made of special materials. The one
finally chosen was made of clay-coated newsboard, shaped into a
carton and lined with a special paper to keep the contents fresh.

As the cake mixes would go to stores all over the country, the
research department had to be sure that the packages would
stand up well during lengthy journeys. They devised a "railroad
boxcar traveling over a desert." This was a machine that would
give the cake mixes the equivalent of a rough twenty-four hour
ride on a fast-moving train at a temperature of about 135 degrees.
The mixes survived the trip well, proving that the containers
were strong and durable enough to protect the product for many
months. Today's cooks can get mixes to make almost any kind of
cake. Some of them, like the various snacking cake mixes, are so
easy to use that there is no need for bowls and beaters—and no
messy clean-up job to do after the cake has been put into the
oven.

During this time, the research kitchens became aware that not
only adults but many girls and boys liked to cook and bake. They

began to take young cooks with the seriousness they deserved. In 1957, *Betty Crocker's Cook Book for Boys and Girls,* a cookbook especially designed for young people, made its appearance. It was followed by other cookbooks that included tempting recipes for cakes and cookies that even the youngest baker could make without help from grownups. Among the most popular are *Candies, Cookies, and Cakes,* by Aileen Paur, and *The Fannie Farmer Junior Cook Book.*

thirteen
What's in a Cake Name?

Cakes have been given all sorts of names, some of them mysterious, like Spider Cake, which does not look like a spider and certainly has no spiders in it. Parkin, too, is a puzzler, although the cake, made of oatmeal and treacle, is an everyday cake in England.

Some cooks simply called their cakes after the baking pan or the way they were made—skillet, cup, funnel, upside-down, refrigerator, and many others. A lot of our favorites are named after an important ingredient in them—spice, walnut, sour cream, raisin.

In the past, making a cake was a project that called for time and energy. Many recipes started with, "Separate your eggs and beat for five hours." When the cook's wrist started to ache, other members of the family had to help with the beating. When a cook found a speedier way of making a cake, she would call it Lightning Cake, Hurry-up Caramel, or One-Two-Three-Four Cake.

Some cakes, like Polly Dole's cake, took their names from the persons who created them. Polly, it seems, was a New England spinster who was disappointed in love. Day after day, Polly wept into her cake batter, yet she made the most delicious cakes in the country. Neighbors begged for the recipe, but the list of ingredients she used only came to light after her death—1½ cups molasses, 1½ cups butter, 1 teaspoon soda, 1 lb. raisins or currants, 1 cup sugar, 4 eggs, 5 cups flour, spices to suit taste.

In Bath, England, a pastrycook named Sally Lunn used to cry her cake in the streets. Damel, a famous baker, bought the recipe from her and named the cakes Sally Lunns.

Grandmothers have long been appreciated for their home-made cakes. Usually, the grandchildren have kept the recipes a secret. But in a little book titled *Chocolate!* Nika Standen Hazleton gives the recipe for My Great-Great-Grandmother's Chocolate Almond Torte. The jealously guarded recipe comes from Germany and goes back to 1842. Dark, rich, and not too sweet, this cake was invariably served when important gentlemen came to dinner. Its original name was Gentleman's Chocolate Cake.

Some cakes have names that start you wondering. Who but a cannibal would enjoy Moors' Heads or Cat's Tongues? Actually, both kind are irresistible. Moors' Heads are covered with dark chocolate icing, filled with hazelnut cream, and baked in special little half-round molds. They were the specialty of a famous bakery in St. Louis, Missouri. Thousands were eaten daily at *Kaffeeklatsches,* social gatherings where ladies met to drink coffee, eat cakes, and talk. Cat's Tongues are delicate wafers, chocolate-coated on one side and shaped like a cat's tongue.

Cakes adopted from other countries often have exciting names. Devil's Pills, from Hungary, are a blend of grated chocolate, candied peel, and sugar. Peppernuts, the German *Pfeffernusse,* are spicy little cakes, about as large as a horse chestnut. At least one cake got its name from a mistake in translation. Petticoat tails, which were sliced from a long roll and kept cold until firm, were taken from France to Scotland by Mary, Queen of Scots. Their French name was *Petits Gâteaux Tailles,* meaning "little cakes cut off," but the Scottish people could not pronounce this. The cakes were named as they sounded—petticoat tails.

Chocolate mixed with carrots may not sound appetizing, but in Vienna, Austria, *Karottentorte* is a great favorite. In it, chocolate is mixed with grated carrot and other ingredients to make a mouth-watering cake. Tutti-frutti (all fruits), as the name suggests, is an Italian summer fruitcake.

Nature has suggested some pretty cake names. Sunshine Cake, as you might expect, is light and golden; so is Daffodil Cake. The shape of a cake sometimes provides a name such as ladyfingers, jelly roll, and the lambs, bunnies, and Santas baked for Easter and Christmas festivities.

Cakes are also named in honor of people, states, cities, and hotels (Lady Baltimore, Nevada Dark Chocolate, Dundee, Waldorf). Sometimes the name-givers seem guilty of discrimination; there are, for example, cakes named after girls (Marguerite, Madelaine, Charlotte), but seldom are cakes named after boys. Johnnycake is really journeycake and is one of our earliest American cakes. The Indians taught the white settlers how to parch corn, mix it with hot water, and make flat, thin cakes. These were carried by hunters and traders on their long journeys on foot over Indian trails. Sometimes mashed pumpkin was mixed into the cakes.

Author Bronwen O'Connor found an old story that explains the name of a special cake that appears in England at Easter time. Once upon a time there lived a poor old couple named Simon and Nell. One day, the neighborhood children came asking for cake, but the old couple had nothing but a piece of dough and the remains of a Christmas pudding.

"What shall we do?" asked Simon.

"Put the pudding in the dough and bake it."

"Boil it, you mean."

"No, it should be baked."

"Don't be silly, boil the thing!"

"It must be baked."

The boil-bake argument went from bad to worse, until Simon and Nell began to throw the furniture at each other. Nell threw a stool that broke against the wall. Simon threw a broom, and missed. Nell threw a couple of eggs.

After a while they calmed down. They collected the broken wood and made a fire. They put the pudding in the dough. They boiled it and *then* baked it. And they used the broken eggs to glaze the top. The cake thus invented became known as a Sim-Nell, or simnel, cake and was later decorated with little balls of marzipan for an Easter treat.

fourteen
Old and New Recipes

If you have already done some baking, you will be at home with these interesting recipes. If you are a beginning baker, adult help may be needed. IT IS ALWAYS ADVISABLE TO HAVE ADULT SUPERVISION WHEN WORKING AROUND THE STOVE OR ON OTHER HOT PROJECTS.

Honey Cakes

1½ cups (355 milliliters) honey
3 tablespoons (42.5 grams) butter
2 tablespoons (28 grams) grated lemon rind
2 teaspoons (10 grams) cinnamon
Pinch each of cloves and allspice
3 cups (681 grams) wheat flour
2 tablespoons (28 grams) baking powder

Preheat oven to 350°. Mix honey and butter in a large saucepan and heat until butter melts. Stir this mixture well, and add spices and lemon rind. Sift two cups of flour with the baking powder, and add to the liquid. Beat well. Add the other cup of flour, mix well, and set the dough aside for several hours or overnight. Pat the dough into 2 greased cake pans. The dough should be about ⅜-inch thick. Bake in a moderate oven for 20 minutes. Cut into bars and remove from pan while still warm. Makes about 2 dozen cakes that keep well in sealed tins.

70

Date-Nut Squares

2 eggs
½ cup (114 grams) sugar
½ teaspoon (2.5 milliliters) vanilla
½ cup (114 grams) all-purpose flour
½ teaspoon (2.5 grams) salt
½ teaspoon (2.5 grams) baking powder
1 cup (227 grams) dates, cut up
½ cup (114 grams) chopped nuts

Preheat oven to 350°. Beat eggs until light and lemon-colored.
Beat in sugar and vanilla thoroughly. Blend in dry ingredients.
Stir in dates and nuts. Spread the batter into a greased and
floured 9 x 9 x 2-inch pan. Bake in a moderate oven for 25 to 30
minutes. Cool; cut into 3-inch squares, and dust with confectioners' sugar if you wish. Makes about 16 squares.

Seed Cake

1 cup (227 grams) butter
1 cup (227 grams) sugar
½ teaspoon (2.5 milliliters) vanilla or almond extract
4 eggs, beaten
2 cups (454 grams) cake flour
¼ teaspoon (1.3 grams) salt
¼ teaspoon (1.3 grams) cream of tartar
1 teaspoon (5 grams) caraway seeds
¼ cup (57 grams) shaved citron
½ teaspoon (2.5 grams) grated lemon rind

Preheat oven to 325°. Cream butter until very light. Gradually add sugar and beat until fluffy. Add flavoring, then eggs, one at a time. Beat vigorously after each addition. Sift and add flour, salt, and cream of tartar. Add caraway seeds, citron, and lemon rind, and mix well. Bake in a greased loaf pan in a moderate oven for about 1 hour.

72

Old Fashioned Spice Cake

4 tablespoons (57 grams) butter
1 cup (227 grams) sugar (can be ½ white, ½ brown)
1 beaten egg
½ cup (118 milliliters) buttermilk
1½ cups (341 grams) flour
1 teaspoon (5 grams) baking soda
½ teaspoon (2.5 grams) cinnamon
½ teaspoon (2.5 grams) nutmeg
pinch salt
1 teaspoon (5 milliliters) vanilla
3 cups (681 grams) tart cooking apples, peeled and diced
½ cup (114 grams) raisins
½ cup (114 grams) chopped nuts

Preheat oven to 350°. Cream butter and sugar. Add egg. Mix dry ingredients, and add to creamed mixture. Stir in vanilla, apples, nuts, and raisins. Pour into two 8-inch greased and floured cake pans and bake for about 40 minutes in a moderate oven. Put the layers together with sweetened whipped cream.

A Name Day Cake

½ cup (118 milliliters) rich milk or cream
1 package powdered yeast
¼ cup (59 milliliters) warm water
2 cups (454 grams) cake flour
¼ lb. (114 grams) butter
5 tablespoons (70 grams) sugar
Salt
Grated rind of one lemon
4 eggs
½ cup (114 grams) raisins
½ cup (114 grams) almonds, chopped
1 teaspoon (5 milliliters) vanilla

Preheat oven to 350°. Dissolve yeast in warm water and set aside. Beat butter until creamy. Add eggs, sugar, and yeast mixture. Then add cream and chopped almonds. Beat well. Stir in flour. Add lemon rind and raisins. Mix well again. Put mixture into greased and preheated fluted pan. Put in warm place, and let rise to about double size. Bake about one hour in moderate oven. Let cake stand for 15 minutes, then remove from pan, and sprinkle with sugar while still warm.

Easter Wafers

These wafers provide a delicious solution to the egg yolks left over from holiday baking. The recipe can easily be doubled to use the egg yolks left from baking an angel cake.

½ cup (114 grams) butter
½ cup (114 grams) sugar
4 egg yolks
Grated rind and juice of 1 lemon
2 cups (454 grams) all purpose flour
¼ teaspoon (1.3 grams) salt

Preheat oven to 350°. Cream butter, salt, and sugar. Add alternately one egg yolk and a portion of the lemon mixture, and beat well. Add flour and mix well. Chill. Put batter on floured board, roll to ¼-inch thickness, and cut with round cookie cutter. Place on a well greased baking sheet and bake for 8 to 10 minutes. Makes about 3 dozen wafers.

76

Minty's Fruitcake (Very easy!)

2 cups (227 grams) self-rising flour
1 cup (227 grams) sugar
½ cup (114 grams) mixed dried fruit (raisins, apricots, apples, etc., cut into small pieces)
2 eggs
¼ lb. (114 grams) butter, melted but not oily
¼ teaspoon (1.5 grams) mixed spice
¼ teaspoon (1.5 grams) ground nutmeg
1 cup (237 milliliters) milk
pinch of salt
a few drops of vanilla

Preheat oven to 325°. Put all ingredients into a large mixing bowl. Beat everything together for 5 minutes with a wooden spoon or for 2 minutes with an electric mixer. Spoon the mixture into a greased cake tin and smooth the top. Bake for 2 hours. Let cake cool. With a knife, ease the sides of the cake from the pan all the way down. Put a cake rack on top of the cake and turn the whole thing upsidedown. Leave the cake to get cold.
Note: If you eat it soon after baking, it will be crumbly and hard to cut, but if you leave it for several hours, it will be much firmer.

77

Old Fashioned Tea Cakes

2 whole eggs
2 cups (454 grams) sugar
1 cup (237 milliliters) buttermilk
1 teaspoon (5 grams) soda
¾ cup (174 grams) shortening
5½ cups (1 kilogram) flour
1 teaspoon (5 grams) salt
1 teaspoon (5 milliliters) vanilla flavoring

Preheat oven to 375°. Combine flour, sugar, and salt in a large mixing bowl. Make a hole in the center of the mixture and put in eggs, shortening, buttermilk, soda, and vanilla flavoring. Mix gradually and thoroughly with the dry ingredients. Chill the dough for 1 hour. Then roll dough ¾ inch thick on a well-floured board. Cut cakes with a biscuit cutter. Place in a greased cake pan and bake for 10 minutes. Makes from six to seven dozen cakes.

Sugar Balls

½ lb. (227 grams) butter or margarine
½ cup (114 grams) confectioners' sugar
2¼ cups (½ kilogram) all-purpose flour
1 teaspoon (5 milliliters) vanilla
1 cup (227 grams) crushed walnuts

Preheat oven to 350°. Cream butter and sugar. Add small amount of flour at a time. Blend all ingredients, mix well. Roll into little balls. Place on a ungreased cokie sheet, and bake for about 15 minutes. While they are still warm, sift more confectioners' sugar over them. Makes about 4 dozen cookies.

Dutch Apple Cake

2 cups (454 grams) sliced cooking apples
½ cup (114 grams) brown sugar
2-4 tablespoons (29-58 grams) butter or margine, melted
1¼ cups (284 grams) all-purpose flour
1¼ teaspoons (6.3 grams) baking powder
¼ teaspoon (1.3 grams) salt
¾ cup (171 grams) sugar
1 egg, well beaten
½ cup (118 milliliters) milk
1 teaspoon (5 milliliters) vanilla
¼ cup (57 grams) butter or margarine

Heat oven to 350°. Arrange apple slices in greased 8-inch pan. Sprinkle with brown sugar. Pour melted butter over apples and sugar. Sift together flour, baking powder, and salt. Then add sugar. Blend egg, milk, and vanilla, and combine with first mixture. Stir in ¼ cup melted butter, and beat vigorously about one minute. Pour this batter over the apple slices, and bake in moderate oven for 45 to 50 minutes. Remove from oven, and immediately loosen cake from sides of pan with spatula. Turn upside down onto plate.

Almond Cheesecakes

¼ pound (114 grams) shelled, ground almonds
3 eggs
¼ cup (57 grams) soft butter
1 cup (227 grams) sugar
½ teaspoon (2.5 milliliters) lemon juice and
   ½ teaspoon (2.5 milliliters) vanilla
6 unbaked 4-inch tart shells

Preheat oven to 325°. Grind almonds in small container of electric blender or use a nut grinder. (Almonds can be chopped with a knife.) Beat eggs until light and fluffy. Add butter, sugar, and flavorings. Add almonds and blend thoroughly. Divide among tart shells. Bake 20 to 25 minutes or until cakes are puffy and set.

Old Favorite Molasses Cake

¼ cup (57 grams) butter
½ cup (114 grams) sifted brown sugar
3 eggs
½ cup (118 milliliters) molasses
2 cups (454 grams) cake flour
1 teaspoon (5 grams) baking soda
¼ teaspoon (1.5 grams) nutmeg
¼ teaspoon (1.5 grams) ground cloves
1 cup (237 milliliters) milk
1 teaspoon (5 milliliters) vanilla

Preheat oven to 350°. Cream butter and sugar. Beat in eggs. Add molasses. Sift flour, soda, and spices together. Add the dry ingredients to the butter, sugar, and egg mixture alternately with milk and vanilla. Bake in a large greased loaf pan in a moderate oven for 45 minutes.

83

Crumb and Nut Cake

1 cup (227 grams) butter or shortening
1 cup (227 grams) sugar
4 eggs
3 cups (681 grams) fine graham cracker crumbs
2 teaspoons (10 milliliters) vanilla
1 cup (227 grams) finely chopped nuts
3 teaspoons (15 grams) baking powder
1 cup (237 milliliters) milk

Preheat oven to 350°. Blend shortening, sugar, eggs, and vanilla. Combine crumbs, nuts, and baking powder, and add to the shortening mixture alternately with milk. Pour into two greased 8-inch cake pans 1¼ inches deep. Bake in a moderate oven for 30 minutes. Turn out on rack to cool. This cake is delicious plain or served with sweetened whipped cream, or you may put the layers together with frosting if you prefer.

Easy Doughnuts

¼ cup (57 grams) melted butter
1 cup (227 grams) sugar
2 eggs, well beaten
4 cups (908 grams) all-purpose flour
1 tablespoon (15 grams) baking powder
½ teaspoon (2.5 grams) each of nutmeg and cinnamon
1 cup (237 milliliters) milk

Cream butter and sugar. Stir in eggs. Mix and sift dry ingredients, and add alternately with milk. Turn on to well-floured board, and roll out about ½-inch thick. Cut with doughnut cutter. Cook a few at a time in large, heavy iron kettle or skillet in deep, hot fat (350° to 375°—be sure to have adult help with this). Turn doughnuts as soon as they rise to the top of the fat. Drain on soft paper towels, and sprinkle with powdered sugar. Makes about 3 dozen doughnuts.

Gingerbread Men

1 cup (227 grams) brown sugar
1 cup (237 milliliters) molasses
1 cup (227 grams) butter or shortening
1 teaspoon (5 grams) baking soda
1 tablespoon (15 grams) ginger
2 eggs
1½ teaspoons (7.5 grams) salt
2 teaspoons (10 grams) baking powder
4-5 cups (900 grams to 1 kilo) flour
¼ cup (59 milliliters) water

Preheat oven to 350°. Mix the first three ingredients in a saucepan and heat to the boiling point. Add soda and ginger. Stir until dissolved. Cool. Add eggs and beat well. Then add dry ingredients alternately with water. Store in refrigerator several hours or overnight. Roll dough thin and cut with a floured gingerbread-man cutter or make a pattern of your own. Make eyes, nose, mouth, buttons, with raisins. Spread on cookie sheet. Bake in a moderate oven for about 10 minutes or until done, according to their thickness.

Gingerbread

2 cups (454 grams) all-purpose flour
1 teaspoon (5 grams) baking soda
1½ teaspoons (7.5 grams) ground ginger
Pinch of cinnamon
Pinch of salt
Pinch of mixed spice
½ cup (118 milliliters) milk
1 cup (227 grams) sugar
½ cup (114 grams) butter or margarine
½ cup (118 milliliters) dark molasses
2 eggs

Preheat oven to 350°. Sift together the flour, soda, salt, and spices. Put milk, sugar, molasses, and butter in a saucepan. Heat until melted, but do not allow to become very hot. Pour melted mixture over the flour mixture; beat well. Add lightly beaten eggs. Beat until mixture is smooth and is the consistency of a thick batter. Pour into greased cake pan, and bake for about 35 minutes in a moderate oven.

Chocolate Pear Cake

1 package chocolate fudge Snackin' Cake mix
1 16-ounce can (474 milliliters) sliced pears
Whipped cream, sweetened

Preheat oven to 350°. Prepare cake mix according to directions, using round 9 x 1½-inch layer pan. Drain can of pears and arrange slices in spoke fashion on batter. Bake 38 to 42 minutes until top springs back when touched lightly in center. Cool. Serve with sweetened whipped cream.

Chocolate Sundae Cake

1 package chocolate fudge Snackin' Cake mix
1 quart (1 liter) ice cream
1 small can chocolate syrup

Preheat oven to 350°. Prepare cake mix according to directions on package. Pour into ungreased 9-inch pie pan. Bake until top springs back when touched lightly in center, 20 to 25 minutes. Cool completely. Cut into wedges. Top with ice cream and drizzle with chocolate syrup.

Little Fruitcakes

1 package applesauce raisin Snackin' Cake mix
1 cup (227 grams) mixed candied fruit
½ cup (114 grams) chopped pecans

Preheat oven to 350°. Prepare the applesauce raisin cake mix as directed on package EXCEPT—MIX IN A BOWL. Stir in mixed candied fruit and chopped pecans. Pour batter into greased muffin cups, filling each about one-half full. Bake until wooden toothpick inserted in center comes out clean, about 25 minutes. Cool 10 minutes. Remove from pan. Cool completely. This recipe makes 16 to 18 fruitcakes.

S'more Cake

1 cup (227 grams) graham cracker crumbs
¼ cup (57 grams) brown sugar (packed)
½ teaspoon (2.5 grams) cinnamon
¼ cup (57 grams) butter or margarine, melted
1 package chocolate fudge Snackin' Cake mix
1½ cups (341 grams) miniature marshmallows

Preheat oven to 350°. Mix crumbs, sugar, cinnamon, and butter.
Prepare cake mix as directed EXCEPT—MIX IN A BOWL. Pour
half of the batter into an ungreased square pan, 8 x 8 x 2 inches.
Sprinkle with crumb mixture. Pour remaining batter over crumb
mixture. Bake 30 minutes. Arrange marshmallows in single layer
on cake. Bake until marshmallows are puffy and light brown, 5 to
7 minutes. Dip knife in water to prevent sticking while cutting.

Banana-Walnut Strawberry Shortcake

1 package banana-walnut Snackin' Cake mix
1 1½-ounce envelope (42.5 grams) whipped topping mix
2 cups (454 grams) sweetened strawberry halves

Preheat oven to 350°. Grease and flour square pan, 8 x 8 x 2 inches. Prepare cake mix as directed on package. Bake 33 to 38 minutes until top springs back when touched lightly in center. Immediately remove from pan. Cool completely. Prepare whipped topping mix as directed on package and spread on cake. Spoon strawberries on top of cake. Store in refrigerator.

INDEX

Page numbers in bold type indicate location of recipes.

Ahijah, 16

All Hallows Eve. *See* Halloween

Almond Cheesecakes, **82**

America, 22, 26, 54-56; cake in, 47-50

American cakes, 57-60, 66, 79-83

American Society of Baking Engineers, 21

Angel food cake, 55

Apis, 21

Artemis, 37

Ashcakes, 16-17, 47-48

Ash Wednesday, 27-29

Austria, 24-25, 36, 66

Aztec Indians, 25

Babka, 36

Baker, Franklin, 53

Baker, James, 25

Baker, Walter, 56

Baking powder, development of, 52

Banana-Walnut Strawberry Shortcake, **93**

"Beans of the Dead," 30

Bible lands, 16-18, 24

Bicentennial cake, 38

Biscuits, beaten, 48-49

Birthday cakes, 33-38

Birthday celebrations: during the Dark Ages, 35; early Christian attitude toward, 35-36; for Egyptian pharaoh, 35; for Roman emperor, 33, 35; in America, 37-38; in England, 37-38; in Germany, 36-37; in Italy, 38

"Bones of the dead," 30

Bors, Etienne de, 51

Bread, 16-17; for wedding ceremonies, 40

Britain, 21-22

Cake-baking as craft, 59-60

Cake flour, development of, 52

Cake mixes, development of, 61-63; recipes with, **89-93**

Candles, birthday, 36-38

"Casket girls," 51-52

Catherine's Day, St., 32

Cat's Tongues, 65

Cheesecake, 42-43

Chiffon cake, 55

Chinese, 19; Mooncake, 59

Chocolate, 52-53; introduction of, 25-26

Chocolate Pear Cake, **89**

Chocolate Sunday Cake, **90**

Christian holidays, cakes for, 74-76; in

America, 27, 32; in Austria, 32; in
England, 27, 28, 31, 32, 66-67; in
France, 31, 32; in French Canada, 32;
in Germany, 31; in Greece, 27, 28, 31;
in Ireland, 30-31; in Poland, 32; in
Russia, 27, 30, 31; in Scotland, 30; in
Serbia, 27; in Sicily, 32; in Switzer-
land, 31. *See also* names of holidays
Christmas, 21, 30-31, 66
Coconut, 53-54
Columbus, Christopher, 51
Corn, 15
Cornmeal, 51-52
Cortez, Hernando, 25
Cracknels, 16
Crumb and Nut Cake, **79**
Crusaders, 24
Cuba, 53
Cupid, 39

Date-Nut Squares, **71**
Devil's food cake, 56
Devil's Pills, 65-66
Dole, Polly, 65
Doughnuts, 30, 49; Easy, **85**
Dutch Apple Cake, 49, **81**
Dundee Cake, 66

Easter, 27-30, 66, 67; Wafers, **76**
Egypt, 15, 19-20, 35, 36
Elizabeth I, Queen, 24
England, 24, 25, 64, 65
Epiphany Day, 32

Fawkes, Guy, 44-45
Fire, 15
France, 24, 25, 26
Fruitcakes, 21; Little, **91**
Fulvius, 35

Gateau des rois, 32
Germany, 36-37, 39, 49-50, 65, 66
Gingerbread, 42-45, **88**; Men, **87**; in
America, 43-44; in East Indies, 44; in
England, 44-45; in France, 44; in
Holland, 44; in New England, 43-44

Good Friday, 29
Greece, 21, 35, 36-37, 42-43
Gugelhupf, 36

Hadrian, Emperor, 33
Halloween, 30
Hazelton, Nika Standen, 65
Hebrews, 15-18
Honey, 18, 43; Cakes, **70**
Holy Saturday, 29
Horsford, Mary, 59
Hot cross buns, 29
Hundred Dollar Cake, 59
Hungary, 36, 65-66
Hurry-up Cake, 64-65
Hymen, 39

Inglehart, Addison, 52
Indians, 47, 66
Italy, 25, 66
Israel, 16-18, 19

Jelly roll, 54-55
Johnnycake, 66
Jeroboam, 16
Joseph's Day St., 32

Kaffeeklatches, 65
Karottentorte, 66
Krullers, 49
Kuglof, 36

Lady Baltimore Cake, 66
Lebenslicht, 37
Lent, 27-29
Lee, Ralph, 21
Lightning Cake, 64-65
Lunn, Sally, 65

Mary, Queen of Scots, 66
Maryland, 48-49
Marriage ceremonies, cakes for, 39-41;
in ancient Rome, 40; in England,
40-41; in Germany, 39; in Hungary, 40
Martin's Day, St., 32
Massachusetts, 26, 47
Mayflower, The, 43

Michigan, 49
Middle Ages, 23-24, 27-29
Minty's Fruitcake, **77**
Monasteries, 23, 29
Moor's Heads, 65
"Mothering," 27-29
Muhammadans, 24
Museum of Contemporary Crafts, 59-60
Muster Day, 43
Muster Gingerbread, 43
My Great-Great-Grandmother's Choco-
  late Almond Torte, 65

Name Day Cake, 36, **75**
Napfkuchen, 36
Nevada Dark Chocolate Cake, 66
New England, 43-44, 49
Newland, Mary Reed, 30
New Orleans, 51-52
New Year's Day, 27

O'Connor, Bronwen, 66
Old-Fashioned Spice Cake, **73**
Old Favorite Molasses Cake, **83**
Old-Fashioned Tea Cakes, **79**
One-Two-Three-Four Cake, 64-65
Oidhche na Ceapairi, 30-31

Pain Calendeau, 31
Parkin, 44-45, 64
Paska, 29
Patisseurs, 24
Paur, Aileen, 63
Pennsylvania Dutch, 49-50
Persians, 35
Peter, Daniel, 26
Petits fours, 24
Petits Gateaux Tilles (Petticoat Tails),
  66
Pfeffernusse, 66
Pilgrims, 47
Pliny, 43
Polo, Marco, 22
Portugal, 24
Pryor, Molly, 57

Quakers, 50
Queen Elizabeth's Cake, 59

Rameses III, 21
Rombauer, Irma S., 45
Robert E. Lee Cake, 57
Rome, 21, 43

Sacher, Edouard, 24-25
Sachertorte, 25
St. Louis, 55, 65
Savoy Cake, 54
Savoy Hotel, 54
Scotland, 66
Seed Cake, **72**
Sicily, 15
Simmons, Amelia, 48
Simnel Cke, 27-29, 66-67
Smallzreid, Katherine Anne, 49
Smith, Paul, 60
S'More Cake, **92**
Socrates, 42-43
Soul Cakes, 30
Spain, 21, 24, 25, 26
Spicer, Dorothy, 59
Spices, introduction of, 21-22
Spider Cake, 64
Sponge Cake, 54-55
Stollen, 37
Stone Age, 51
Sugar, 51; Balls, **80**; first use of, 24
Switzerland, 26
Sykes, John, 41

Thearion, 15
Tiddy Doll, 44
Tutti-frutti, 66

Van Rensseler, Mrs., 49
Virginia, 48

Waldorf Cake, 66
Washington, Martha, 48
West Indies, 51, 53
Wedding cakes, 39-41; cheesecakes as,
  43
Weeden, Howard, 49
William the Conqueror, 44
Worship, Egyptian use of cake in, 19-20

Xanthippe, 43